Gabriel's Horn

Readers' Theater
For Advent

Frank Ramirez

CSS Publishing Company, Inc., Lima, Ohio

GABRIEL'S HORN

For more information about CSS Publishing Company resources, visit our website at
www.csspub.com or e-mail us at custserv@csspub.com or call (800) 241-4056.

Cover design by Barbara Spencer
ISBN 0-7880-2385-3   PRINTED IN U.S.A.

Dedicated to
Bill McMillin (Gabriel)
Alyssa Harclerode (Wonderful)
Kasey Leidy (Marvelous)
for saying, "Yes," when I asked
them to take part in this cycle.

Table Of Contents

Introduction

In 2002, I wrote a short play called "M.I.H. — Missing In Heaven" for an Easter Sunrise service published by CSS in *Roll Back The Stone*. In the play, the Angel Gabriel has taken a 33-year vacation since the birth of Jesus and upon his return sets out to discover what happened in his absence. He is assisted by the Angel Wonderful, who rounds up a number of animals and objects who tell the story of the ministry, arrest, death, and resurrection of Jesus.

Between Lent and Advent of that year, I changed homes, churches, and states, but not Saviors, so I decided to write a whole sequence for the Christmas season, beginning with the Last Sunday Of Pentecost, and continuing through the Fourth Sunday In Advent. The Advent Wreath was presented a week early, though the candles were not lit, and each play followed the lighting of the Advent Wreath. A litany and a hymn were included in the sequence as well. I preached on the following texts:

> Last Sunday Of Pentecost: Matthew 25:31-46
> First Sunday In Advent: Genesis 12:1-9
> Second Sunday In Advent: Haggai 1:1-9
> Third Sunday In Advent: Nehemiah 8:1-12
> Fourth Sunday In Advent: Luke 1:26-38

(Haggai might seem a strange choice for an Advent message, but one of my books, *Coming Home*, published by CSS, includes seven sermons for the Christmas season built around that obscure prophet.)

The plays were costumed in what I call "Basic Bible Bathrobe." We altered two white choir robes for Wonderful and Marvelous, who were played by two junior high students, and the Angel Gabriel fashioned himself a robe out of a bedsheet. All three wore a gold or silver tinsel garland around the head for a halo. Gabriel's horn was a red construction paper tube, and the sound was provided by the organist. The other characters were dressed in whatever colorful robes and headpieces we had in the church basement set aside for various pageants.

The plays were performed in Readers' Theater style. The actors stood before microphones with their scripts in hand. They read

7

through them aloud a couple of times in rehearsal to work out pronunciation and cadence. The plays are not serious in tone, and the meter with rhyme is intended to reflect this.

In the play "The Reading Club" Gabriel uses two terms that may be unfamiliar to some. *Qoholeth* is a transliteration of the name or title of the author of Ecclesiastes. You might say Solomon instead (although I don't think Solomon wrote the book). As for *tohu v'bohu*, that's the phrase from Genesis 1:2 that is often translated "formless void" or "formless and empty," and is a personification of the chaos that God controls. I'd pronounce it "tow-hoo v'bow-hoo," with emphasis on the tow and bow. That's a "bow" as in bow tie and not in bowwow.

The final play, "Step Up To The Plate," concludes with a simple Christmas pageant. You might refer to my "The 'Did Someone Forget To Plan' The Christmas Pageant!" in the CSS publication *The Christmas Star: Readings and Pageants for Christmas*.

As for the names of the angels, I named one angel Wonderful because of the way my fancy was tickled on reading Judges 13:18 in the Revised Standard Version (And the angel of the LORD said to him, "Why do you ask my name, seeing it is wonderful?"). When I wrote this cycle I decided if an angel could be named Wonderful, another could be called Marvelous.

So far I've never experienced two Christmas seasons the same, despite the fact that we are retelling the same wonderful story. My prayer is that you may be blessed through the use of these little plays as in a roundabout fashion you come back to the place you had started from, telling the story of salvation for the first time, once more, all over again.

Gabriel's Horn

Characters
Angel Marvelous
Angel Wonderful
Angel Gabriel

(The scene is heaven and two Angels enter.)

Marvelous
Welcome to heaven. Have you been away?

Wonderful
I've been off working. What can I say?
How about you? I think I kinda know you
Like someone I met.

Marvelous
It might have been below you.
I'm often assigned to duty in the field,
The work of the Lord, sending messages twice sealed,
Or directing the traffic of the birds in their flight
And sometimes the stars as they soar through the night.
And you, where on earth or in heaven, might I
Have run into you, buddy?

Wonderful
On business I fly
Where I'm sent, with a mission I'm lent, never bored.
On the winds of God's word I have flown, I have soared.

Marvelous
My name is Marvelous. Hey, I didn't choose it.
When it's printed on T-shirts or mugs I don't lose it.

9

Wonderful
My name is Wonderful. I was the messenger
Who told Samson's mother a baby would share
Her home though for long there was no baby blessing her,
But her son was special. Just don't cut his hair.

Marvelous
I think I remember that fuss and that bother.
Did that make the Bible?

Wonderful
Take one. You need it.
You can learn all about it in Judges.

Marvelous
Some other
Millennium when I slow down I might read it.
For now I've been busy.

Wonderful
Did you visit a prophet?

Marvelous
No, an Archangel's coming! A big wig I heard!

Wonderful
Where'd it go? Here's my hat. Do you think I should doff it?

Marvelous
Oh, please. He's an angel like us. That's absurd.
(Enter Gabriel with long horn.)
And who are you, creature of luminous light?

Gabriel
My name is Gabriel. My head is shorn
Of halo or hat, but I still have this horn.
I come from the most august throne at the center

Of all that is holy while down below winter
Is raging, assaulting on all the five senses.
Meanwhile in Israel they've got the census
And each to a hometown must go to be counted,
Arriving on foot, or on stern donkey mounted.
There's plenty of tension across the old empire
I think that it's time for the light from the lamp. Fire
Spread from the corners of this tired globe
And burn away dross, leaving only the precious —

Wonderful
Excuse me. Hey you in the natty white robe!

Marvelous
I don't think he heard us. This could get delicious.

Gabriel
It's time that I blew on my horn, the last trump!

Wonderful
Who told you to do so this morn? Not the ump!

Gabriel
I'm the angel recording the times and the seasons.
When I say it's over, it's over. No reasons
Are needed. I've looked at this dark, wicked earth
And seen there's a lack, there's a definite dearth
Of good will to all. There is sin here to mop
Up and wash away. Blow, my horn!

Marvelous and Wonderful
Stop!

Marvelous
There's more to be offered. The world has grown colder.

Wonderful
The Ancient of Days, though, is not one hour older.
A day like a thousand of years quickly passes.

Marvelous
And sure, everything fades away like the grasses
But something endures, a plan we can follow
That comes from the Father that all may still hallow.

Gabriel
That bit about grass fading's fine. Why, may, ah,
I quote from it?

Marvelous
Sure. From the prophet —

Wonderful
Isaiah

Marvelous
I think so.

Gabriel
Then all flesh is grass and let all, low and great,
Fade when I blow on this trumpet here.

Wonderful
Wait!
You're going to end all of history now?

Gabriel
It's seems like the right time, so don't have a cow.
The world's in a mess, and it's not getting better.
Try getting a room. It's cold. Get a sweater.
Nobody makes room for the ones who, in need,
Are wandering aimlessly.

Marvelous
Yet, in the reed
And the billowing wave of the marsh floated Moses
Remember the time Pharaoh's daughter his toeses
And fingers were counting and raised up a prophet
Despite all the doubters who, tempted to scoff it,
Cried aloud to cross back and be slaves once again.
There are many around still enslaved — but to sin!

Wonderful
It's somewhere or other still inside these pages,
I'm sure that I read it, that one of these sages
Said a Savior is coming, a prophet much greater
Than Moses —

Gabriel
— Not Moses —

Marvelous
And yet, like a waiter
In meekness and service, not glory and power,
He'll save all creation.

Gabriel
Still, this is the hour
This horn I will blow. I won't wait no longer.

Wonderful
Your negative's double, and I'm a belonger
To grammar that's proper.

Marvelous
That means you must pause
And allow us to show you in scripture the cause
For hope in the midst of this sad, sinful world
That a much greater plan might still be unfurled.

Wonderful
(holds up Bible)
Besides every prophet in much of this book
Has pointed to one greater still. Take a look!
And remember whatever the warning they say
They all add an "if" and insist a delay
Must be given so people can finally repent.

Gabriel
Fine. You've convinced me. For now I'll relent.
This horn will stay near, but to me you must show
Examples from history so I might know
There's hope in God's people, despite the appearance
Of failure, fire, and fickle adherence
To all of the chances that they have been given.

Marvelous and Gabriel
Hip hooray! And now we'll start livin'.

Gabriel
Each week travel with us through biblical time
Discovering in both our prose and our rhyme
How servants of God when asked would fulfill
The Almighty's wishes and do his good will.

The Honeymooners

Characters
Angel Marvelous
Angel Wonderful
Angel Gabriel
Abram
Sarai

(Enter the angels Marvelous, Wonderful, and Gabriel with his horn.)

Gabriel
You can say all you want, but I told you before
With this horn and my lungs I can bring down the curtain
On history, leaving the rich and the poor
To answer the summons.

Wonderful
Maybe. One thing's still certain.
Before it all ends we would like you to see
That from the beginning of our history
God's people have given their best, certainly.

Marvelous
I know that the kingdom to come will be great,
But millions of souls need a chance, so please wait.
There are autumns to cherish and summers to nourish
And winters to scour and springs with a flourish
To call back to life everything that is good
So God's faithful people can plant and grow food.

Wonderful
There's so much to see with our wings we might wander
And see only half. Was it made just to squander?

15

Gabriel
I agree that the wonders of blessed creation
Are more than magnificent, mighty, but moot.
Instead you might show anyone from this nation
Who's faithfully lived on this planet, to boot.

Marvelous
There's plenty of people ...

Wonderful
That make good examples
For you to consider.

Gabriel
I'd like a few samples.

Wonderful
I'm thinking of Samson, as strong as the truth,
Or how about someone as faithful as Ruth?

Gabriel
That goes for the youngest. That goes for the bold.
That goes for the strongest, but not for the old.
The ones who the longest have lived had a blessing
Of manifold wisdom, or so I am guessing.
You'd think that the faith of the ones who have seen
Both good and bad seasons would be quite serene.

Marvelous
We're glad that you brought up the matter of age.

Wonderful
For here by the oaks we call Mamre a sage
And his spouse are about to embark on a stage
Of living reserved for the young.

Marvelous
Turn the page
Of the Bible. Discover that they're all the rage.

Gabriel
Why that's Abram and Sarai if I rightly gauge.

(Abram and Sarai enter.)

Abram
My Sarai, you're quiet. This isn't like you.
You're normally talkative. What can I do?
Can I make you a cake?

Sarai
Hardly, honey. You're not
A cook by the nook of your shepherd's crook. Hot
Or cold, tepid, torpid, fully cooked, wholly raw
You're by far the best shepherd and worst cook I saw.

Abram
Well, what then? It's obvious you're out of sorts.

Gabriel
She's honest, but does she put starch in his shorts?

Marvelous
Why ask?

Gabriel
Just because of the way this guy walks.

Wonderful
Hey! Everyone quiet while both of them talks.

Sarai
I know it's too late and of course I'm so tired.
I've never been pregnant and you never sired.
How sad, my dear husband, we never had kids.

Abram
Well maybe, my Sarai, but my heavy lids
Make it clear that I'm far too old and too sleepy
To raise any children. So please don't get weepy
The way that you do when our neighbor's loud brats
Go play on our doorstep with all their noise.

Gabriel
Rats!
It's just like I told you. These people don't care.
Just hand them a coat when the weather turns cold
And feed them on time and enough they can share.
And anything else? They'll just say they're too old.

Marvelous
Do you have a fire in the seat of your pants?

Wonderful
Just calm down and listen and give them a chance.

Abram
I'm glad at the least that we're settled. This house
Is homelike enough.

Sarai
Perhaps. I'm a louse
To bring this up once again. Still, I'm your spouse.
I'd give up this house, and all that you see
Our livelihood, yes, and our security
If a child were ours.

Abram
Blimey, Faith and Begorrah
I'm glad we're in Haran and not in Gomorrah
At our time of life to be parents? It's certain
Our heads would be aching and joints would be hurtin'
And you be a mother? By age you're a granny.

Sarai
Abram, have you never heard of a nanny?
It takes a whole village to raise up a child.
I'm sure we'd have help.

Abram
But some children are wild!
You're thinking of gentle kids, modest and nice.

Sarai
Did you ever find something for that sacrifice
You spoke about Saturday?

Abram
The subject don't change.
Do you think at this time in our lives we'd arrange
For cradles and bottles and nursery toys?

Sarai
I somehow believe God intends for us joys.

(Abram and Sarai exit different directions.)

Gabriel
Well, thank you my friends. My point has been made.
Now where is my trumpet? Yes. There in the shade.
You can say what you want in this slough of despond,
But ask all you want and they just won't respond.

(Abram and Sarai both re-enter.)

19

Abram

Sarai, my Sarai, don't moan and don't kvetch,
And most of all keep all those clothes that still stretch
In the waistband, I've heard the most marvelous word
That comes from none other than he who's the Lord!

Sarai

I heard the same thing, at least that's what I'm thinking
A voice told me, stop all your crying and blinking.
Rise up, O Sarai, and you who's her husband.
Trust in high heaven and please don't you fuss. Sand
In plenty lines shorelines and all your descendants
Will outnumber those and the myriad blamed ants
That spoil the picnics beyond any counting.
You're having a baby someday. Tension's mounting
In all parts of heaven. The angels must know
If because of this favor we're willing to go
Wherever God leads us for years beyond number.
When traveling bring all your goods and encumber
Yourselves with your servants and all of the household
And take all the plumbing and even the mouse.

Abram

Hold
Your tongue for a moment. That's just what I heard
And I take it on faith it's the word of the Lord!

Sarai

So what should we do? Just a moment ago
You said we're too old. Now you think we should go?

Abram

I did say we're settled, and that is for certain

Sarai

And we just got new siding. I picked out a curtain
To go with the kitchen remodeled last summer
And now is the time we should go? What a bummer!

20

Gabriel

I've heard quite enough for this horn to be blowing.

Sarai

But if it's what God wants let's get packed and get going.

Abram

I agree. Let's be off to see where this might lead us.
Let's wake up the household to see if they heed us.
Who knows what this means at this time of our life.
It could be travail. There might be much strife.
It's all quite uncertain, but one thing's for sure.

Sarai

I'll someday be pregnant. The thought I'll endure!

Wonderful

We told you, O Gabriel. No one's too old
To answer God's call. Let your notes be all rolled
Back into your world ending unbending trump

Gabriel

At least until next week. We'll see if you stump
Me when once more I'll seek to bring all to an end.

Marvelous

Just so long as you come when the two of us send.

Wonderful

Let Abram and Sarai be everyone's guide.
No matter how old we might feel inside
Be sure that God loves us and needs us to cover
The strange situations that life will discover.

The Cleanup Crew

Characters
Angel Marvelous
Angel Wonderful
Angel Gabriel
Janitor
God's People (Congregation)

(Enter the angels Marvelous, Wonderful, Gabriel, and Janitor.)

Marvelous
Are you sure that the map that you bought is correct?
I thought that the temple we'd stop and inspect!
We'd see how the people are faithful, deserving
Of more time, of good time. It's God that they're serving!
Don't ring down creation while good people gather.

Gabriel
Just what sort of people? Like old Cotton Mather
Who said he was one of God's chosen, yet while
He cracked down on fun he would not crack a smile?

Wonderful
Now please both relax, keep your halo and shirt on.
The temple should be on this spot, I am certain.
All the same I can't help but be puzzled by sticks
That are scattered around where I'd like to see bricks!
Where is the altar? Where is the stonework?
Just seeing these ruins is making me groan.

Gabriel
Shirk
Your duty no longer. Don't try to impress me
And don't you suggest that among all this mess —

23

Marvelous
See!
There is a person who's pushing a broom.

Gabriel
If I'm not convinced, it's *alarums* and gloom
As I blow on this trumpet and bring to an end
The world. It's a goose on a wild chase we send
By coming to here on this forsaken spot.
I'm sorry to tell you, impressed I am not.

Janitor
Got to clean up, got to work in this rubble.
No time to shave so I've still got a stubble.
Why don't the people who ought to care more
Help to rebuild the old temple and share more
Of substance and service? The reason's not hazy.
I'm really disgusted because some are just lazy.
I know they are busy. Priorities matter.
But why not squeeze service to God in the batter
We bake of our lives? All the people have sinned.
That's why it's dry and the hot blowing wind
Has battered our crops. What is more I am sure
That service to God is a part of the cure.

Wonderful
Hey you, who is wandering here in the ruins
Of what was the temple, where now wild bruins
And beasts from the wilderness howl and haunt,
Please tell us what happened, or else if you can't
Direct us to somebody else who just might.

Janitor
There's really no secret, O creature of light.
I'm just as depressed by this sad, dismal sight.
The crops are not growing, though farmers are sowing
There isn't the rain, so nothing we gain.

I'm trying to warn 'yer, there's nothing to garner
From field or fountain, valley or mountain.
I'm sure it's because we've forgotten the altar
Of regular worship and that's why we falter.

Marvelous
That's exactly the point, and if we don't rouse
These people to once again build up God's house
That very large angel with trumpeting horn
Will call down upon all the earth the dark scorn
Of angels avenging and call to an end
This world of great sadness.

Janitor
How can I defend
A people who won't from their tracks set about?

Wonderful
We need us a prophet, who'll give a great shout!
Will you be that prophet? Will you be the one
Who keeps our friend Gabriel from having his fun?

Gabriel
I doubt it. Although he is nobody's fool
I don't think this man went to propheting school.

Janitor
And not only that, but in just four months' time
I have to be moving on. Is that such a crime?

Marvelous
But who says a prophet must give up a year?

Wonderful
Or many years? No one. Get rid of your fear.
In only four months we could all rearrange
Priorities, get all these people to change!

Marvelous
Just try it. Just cry aloud, warn all these people
They should have been here building up the high steeple,
And hanging the church doors —

Wonderful
This list could get numbing.

Gabriel
I'll put in my spoke and insist upon plumbing.

Janitor
But why would they listen?

Wonderful
Don't settle for art.
Just say what you think and please speak from the heart.

Marvelous
These folks need a prophet and don't even know it.
There are a seed to be planted. Won't you please sow it?
It's just for a couple of months of your trouble
And then you'll be free. Won't you start on the double?

Janitor
(turns to Congregation)
Say, all of you there, who are sitting at ease
As fat and as sassy as each of you please!
Just look all about you, don't take my word for it.
The temple's in ruins. This wall, I must shore it.
There aren't any windows, but clear to the sky
You can see all the birds and the clouds floating by.
I work in the summer and can't stand the heat,
And clean up all winter, just stamping my feet.
Hello, won't you listen? Is anyone there?

God's People
Just give us a reason, for none of us care.
We've errands to run, we've parcels to pack,
The leaves must be raked and someone must stack
The gifts in their boxes this holiday season.
You're asking a lot, without giving a reason!

Janitor
As my name is Haggai, and this is not *my* bull
I'm telling you words that come straight from the Bible.
If you don't want to be like chopped liver in wurst
Then I think that you people must all put God first!
You've lived in your houses all paneled for moons
Beyond measure. This temple is lying in ruins.
I'm waiting, and it's been a great many years
Since you have left Babylon, wiped away tears,
And started a new life in this happy land.
Now ask yourself why this good soil is sand,
And why you buy clothes and yet never feel warm
And eat and drink plenty, yet do yourself harm.
Your money is stuffed in a bag full of holes,
And all of your lawns are invaded by moles!
Think how you have fared, says the great Lord of hosts,
Go up to the hills and bring wood, or you're ghosts.
The Lord should come first, both in this and all seasons.
The fact God is God is the greatest of reasons.

God's People
You're right, and we won't say again that we're busy.
It's time that we all ran about in a tizzy
While working for God. Everyone, old and young
Will shout, sing, and holler, will loosen their tongue.
It's talent we've got, opportunity, time,
And the will to praise God in our prose and our rhyme.
Since God calls we're ready. We'll make no excuses
It's time to sing carols, no need to sing blueses.

Gabriel
Impressive. I guess that will settle for now
If I should the horn blow.

Marvelous
You said it.

Wonderful
And how.
It just took a prophet to rattle the town.
They're no longer lazy.

Gabriel
Take a look at this gown.
Do you think that it flatters me? The truth you must tell.

Marvelous
I'll let you know next week. I hear, like a knell
The temple bell's ringing. These people are working.
They're all acting busy, there's nobody shirking.
And you, please consider, a king will be here.

Wonderful
Enjoy everything in this season. It's clear
There's so much to do, but if you must hurry
Keep your eye on the star and not on the fury.

Gabriel
The words of the prophet called Haggai to all
Beg you not to be busy and miss on God's call.

The Reading Club

Characters
Angel Marvelous
Angel Wonderful
Angel Gabriel
Hannah
Nehemiah

(Enter angels Marvelous, Wonderful, Gabriel, Hannah, and Nehemiah.)

Gabriel
So where are we standing? What place have you brought us?

Marvelous
Right here is the temple.

Gabriel
That's just as I thought.

Wonderful
Fuss
Or not. Take a look at the people around.

Gabriel
They look like they're lost.

Marvelous
Can we help them get found?

Wonderful
They don't have the Bible. There's no one to read it.
There's no one to pray it. There's no one to heed it.

Gabriel
But aren't these God's people, and ain't this the temple?

Marvelous
Instead of an answer I'll give you a sample.
Hey, you there, an otherwise smart-looking girl.
I've got a few questions.

Hannah
I'll give it a whirl.

Marvelous
Are you one of God's people?

Hannah
I follow the Lord.

Wonderful
Then quote if you can just a piece of God's Word.

Hannah
The Word? Any Word?

Marvelous
The Bible's the book
That's filled with the story of love. Take a look.
Have you heard about Moses, the Red Sea, and Pharaoh?

Hannah
It don't sound familiar like someone would share.

Wonderful
Oh!
Then what of creation, the seven days' wonder.

Hannah
I stand at my station and hope I don't blunder.
Creation?

Gabriel
I can't say this sounds at all hopeful.
If she were my pupil, her mouth gets a soap full.

Marvelous
Joshua leads over Jordan, then Judges.
Ruth and Naomi are nobody's drudges.

Wonderful
Proverbs bring wisdom, and nobody fudges
The Psalms, but they pray 'em.

Gabriel
David can meet a great giant and slay 'im.

Marvelous
The Lord is our shepherd it says in a psalm.
Tamar is a hero and also a palm.

Wonderful
Elijah is tired but fed by the birds.

Gabriel
While *Qoholeth* sighs, it's all nothing but words,
And vanity reigns. Everything has a season.

Marvelous
The prophets speak truth and they give us a reason
To think there is hope.

Gabriel
And when God, like the wind,
Hovers over the waters, though the people have sinned,
There is hope, for the chaos, the *tohu v'bohu*,
Is tamed at creation.

Hannah
Excuse me please. Yoo hoo!
It sounds quite appealing, but I never read it.

Wonderful
It's hard to believe, even harder to credit.

Hannah
Please ask me the height of the moon if you're able,
I'll give you instructions on cleaning the stable.
Or how about cooking? I make a mean pita
That I'll fill with fresh lamb and the cheese they call feta.
Write a poem, build an arch, shoe a horse, I'd be liable.
But never have I seen a book called the Bible.

Marvelous
Don't you all think it's a little bit odd
These folks had this treasure, the bright word of God,
And never found time for its use, for the pleasure
Of studying what is a priceless, grand treasure?

Gabriel
I've heard quite enough. The whole thing is crazy.
They don't have a Bible? I say that they're lazy.
There's nothing more precious than God's holy word
Yet this is a thing that they never have heard!
In good times and bad through the myriad years
The people have learned from the sages and seers.
This book has brought comfort to those in distress
And told sinners that there was still time to confess.
Just as Samson lost strength with his cranium shorn,
They're weak without word. I am blowing my horn
And ending the travesty that I'm beholding.

Wonderful
One moment, Archangel.

Marvelous
We still need a bold king
Or prophet remembering Solomon's saws
And help to restore faith in all of God's laws.

Nehemiah
Angels be thanked! Don't sue me for libel
But if I'm correct then I'm holding the Bible
We haven't seen one of these Bibles for years.
We thought we had lost them. That's one of our fears.
Now all — celebrate. Hip hooroo. Happy day!

Hannah
I've only one question.

Nehemiah
Well?

Hannah
What does it say?
In our day and age you can be very smart,
But reading's a specialized technical art.

Nehemiah
My name's Nehemiah, the one that you need.

Hannah
What makes you so special?

Nehemiah
I know how to read.
Not everyone can in this age before schooling.
There's no apples or chalkboards and no golden ruling.
What is more, if you'll listen and not act so proud
I'm happy to read the whole thing here, aloud.

Hannah
We're happy to listen, no matter that we
Might learn that we sinned for the truth sets us free.

Nehemiah
Then gather, all people, the high and the low,
And learn from God's word all the things you should know.
First things are first. Splatter blood and take cover
Because once a year we remember Passover.
No matter that you are behind in your rents
Build booths out of town for the feast of all tents.
There's a Day of Atonement we call Yom Kippur,
That comes near the New Year. Of that I am sure.
And here's Ten Commandments, not nine or eleven.
Just keep them so you can all get into heaven.
And most of all, people, it says here some day
One greater than Moses will show us the way.

Hannah
Boo hoo! And again I say, "Hoo boo ree boo!"
We didn't know what we were all meant to do!
All these years we have failed to honor the Lord
Because no one read to us from out of the word.

Nehemiah
Don't weep and don't mourn if you've missed God's command.
There's time for repentance. In mercy you stand.
You've scars from the past. Tend your wound, close your suture,
Accept God's forgiveness, and look to your future.
In bountiful banquets please gather together,
These good times a foretaste of what lasts forever.

Wonderful
It seems to me clear there's a lesson to learn.
Please open your Bible. Oh, people, please yearn
For the blessings inside. These words you should crave.

Marvelous
It's easy to open and simple to save.

Gabriel
Take a cue from these folks, steal a glance, take a look,
Grab a gander at this, the grandest, this book.
And speaking of which, when's the last time you read it?

Wonderful
It can't be that long ago.

Gabriel
Listen. I've said it
Before and I'll say it again and again.
We angels should read the commandments —

Marvelous
There's ten!

Gabriel
That answer was easy. Now tell me what is
Contained in this book or I'll give you a quiz.

Marvelous
We've a saying, we angels, because we get busy.
We'll tell it you simply. Don't get in a tizzy.

Wonderful
When it comes to the Bible you have time to read it
Unless you're inside it. Then God's will, you speed it.

Gabriel
That's not an excuse. Start right here with verse one,
And read the whole Bible until you are done.

Marvelous and Wonderful
Very well. Like God's people we can't be so stressed
That we won't read God's word because then we'd be blessed.

Step Up To The Plate

Characters
Angel Marvelous
Angel Wonderful
Angel Gabriel
Mary

(Enter Mary and angels Marvelous, Wonderful, and Gabriel.)

Mary
My name is Mary, a common cognomen.
I live here in Nazareth, and in the gloamin'
Watching the sun set, without thought of roamin',
I am content. Why not? I'm engaged
To Joseph, a carpenter. This is my home 'n'
Here in my hometown the wedding is staged.
Marry this man? As a Mary I'm merry
And not in the least bit obtuse or contrary.
I tarry to wed the good man who works wood
As I should when I could, and is well understood.

Gabriel
You brought me posthaste and at no small expense
To the village of Nazareth in Galilee,
Three days from Jerusalem. This makes no sense.
A thirteen-year-old rhymes away, I can see.
So why are we here?

Marvelous
Please do not make a fuss.
It's not just about her. It's all about us.

37

Gabriel

Is there something about her that I need to know?

Wonderful

I guess we should tell you.

Marvelous

This tale of woe
Began with the story of Adam and Eve
Continuing with the poor choices that grieve
The One who had planned everything for the good
If only things happened the way that they should.

Wonderful

But that's in the past, and our God looks ahead
To plan something grand to take place here instead.
The prophets from Moses through sharp Malachi
Have said that a great one will someday come by.
This child born of Mary will carry the sins
To the cross and the grave and beyond. So begins
The healing of harms and the ending of woes.

Gabriel

And we're here together to see how it goes?
This plan sounds fantastic. There's no need to scoff.
I take it we get this girl soon married off.

Marvelous

But first she'll be asked, in sound and in sense,
To bear the Messiah, and if she consents.

Wonderful

This woman will soon make a difficult choice.
But God will not tell her. God gives us a voice
To say yes or no, to put in our spoke.

Gabriel
God still trusts the people? Is this a poor joke?

Marvelous
Though we angels are perfect and creatures of light
And stand without ceasing while praising the sight
Of what is to mortals invisible, still
It's with humans that God takes a gamble and will,
Without hesitation, take chances believing
That love calls to love, as it gives is receiving
That love in return.

Gabriel
Will this girl pass the test?
She's young and she's pretty. But is she the best?
When it comes to the point and she's told will she run?

Wonderful
The Bible says nothing is new 'neath the sun,
And also behold, I am making things new.
Though contrary both words are equally true.

Gabriel
The Almighty might be a risk taker. Still
All things would go smoothly if he had his will.
So what is this choice that you spoke of and why
Would anyone hesitate, given the try?

Marvelous
Well yes, that's the plan, but as history's mergin'
With prophecy there is a roadblock before.
Isaiah once said for a sign that a virgin
Is found with a child. Need I say more?

Gabriel
Boy, what a shocker. You might call me yeller,
But I am so thankful I don't have to tell her.

Wonderful
Yes, that's why we're here, our personal angle,
Is someone must tell her about this great tangle.
The one for the job is a *really big* angel.

Gabriel
Then you go and tell her.

Marvelous
We would if we could
But if we spoke we might be misunderstood.

Gabriel
Hail Mary!

Wonderful
That's catchy. Please write that phrase down.

Marvelous
Is hail a verb in this context or noun?

Gabriel
Hail Mary, again! I'm calling! Hello!
I've come here to tell you a thing you should know.

Mary
I don't know a thing that you angels have said.
That's because I am stunned. Should I say I'm afraid?

Gabriel
Fear not. And here for the lawyers I pause
This plea to fear not is a standard, a clause,
We always give.

Mary
Tell me why.

Gabriel
Oh, just because.
But now to the serious part of this speech.

Wonderful
Speak clearly, don't lecture, and please, don't you preach.

Marvelous
The Lord has found favor in you and you're blessed.

Mary
With angels as visitors, this I have guessed.

Gabriel
Please pay close attention, for you will conceive
In a wonderful manner that's hard to believe.
And you'll bear a son that was sent here to please us.
Immanuel, he will be God with us, Jesus.
Far greater than great, and the Most High One's Son,
With David an ancestor. His reign's begun
And will without ending be present forever!

Mary
Excuse me. I would hate your employment to sever,
But I am a virgin, so how could this be?

Gabriel
The gift of God's Spirit is yours, fair and free.
The Son of God, holy, a gift to the peoples —

Marvelous
Just think of the churches to come, and the steeples!

Wonderful
Just think of the praises and carols and stories
That rest in the future to tell of these glories.

Gabriel
And here is a sign, queen of heaven and regnant.
Your cousin Elizabeth in old age is pregnant.
They said she was barren, but three months from now
She's going to give birth.

Wonderful
And will she!

Marvelous
And how!

Gabriel
Nothing's impossible when it's the will
Of heaven.

Mary
A given. Yet ... so ... even ... still ...

Marvelous
I know that it's hard but you have to be steady.

Mary
That's easy for you but I know I'm not ready.
I know that I have here a choice and not fate.
I still might be willing, but can't you all wait?

Gabriel
The timing's not ours, but the moment is here.
This comes from above and is really quite clear.
I can't claim I know why it's you of all women
But now comes a fisher of people. Start swimmin'.
This child must be born, and God's plan come to pass.
The prophets foretold this event once, my lass.

Mary
You say that a child is in my near future.
Did anyone notice I'm unmarried?

Gabriel
Suit your
Self. But be certain that if you say, "Yes"
Salvation is certain for all time to bless!

Mary
We're none of us ready, there never will be
A moment that's perfect for eternity.
It's never the right time, not nighttime or day
But God's plan will still fill the bill anyway.
Though I think the whole thing is really absurd.
I'm Mary, your servant. Let happen God's word.

Gabriel
Well one thing's for sure now that Mary said sure.
I'm blowing this horn.

Marvelous
Is there really no cure
Or is this a note that we all must endure?

Wonderful
You said you would end all the world in a note
If God was ignored, so you said, quote, unquote.

Marvelous
But we've shown you these samples of those who responded
To calls in the Bible. So aren't you astounded?
Please don't end the world!

Wonderful
We're begging you please!

Gabriel
Oh, take a deep breath and now none of you sneeze!
The tune for time's ending is written in minor
And this is a major, and gentle and finer!
My mood is much lighter and I've no intent
To end the world. No. Now a new tune is sent
To shepherds and kings and kids of all ages,
To prophets and poets and ten kinds of sages.
This Gloria glances off stars to rebound
On grand rims of galaxies!

(The tune "Gloria in Excelsis Deo" is played on the trumpet or on the organ with the trumpet stop.)

Wonderful
That's quite a sound.
Everyone sing, and be sure with the sight
Of the virgin and child that all is all right!

Marvelous
Put the whole world on notice, despite all misgiving,
The Lord of all life calls on all to keep living.
The word is made flesh and will dwell here among
The people, all people, the old and the young.

Gabriel
Never forget that God gives us a call
And trusts we'll respond, in our weakness give all.
Merry Christmas, good will, gloria, *Deo gratias!*
You humans come through in a pinch. Muchas gracias.
Peace on earth, and no dearth of the good will divine
Is showered upon you. Heed here the sign.
The virgin with child in a manger has laid
In swaddling clothes the one who has paid
The price for your sins. Everybody repent!

Marvelous
Save a few of these rhymes for the season of lent.

Gabriel
Merry Christmas to all through the day and the night.
Here comes our fair pageant. Please take in the sight.

(A simple pageant could follow. The scripture texts of Luke 2:1-20 and Matthew 2:1-12 could be read by youth while children enter in costume and take their places. The pageant could conclude with a Christmas carol such as "Away In A Manger.")